I0519099

Living Love Forward

Being Your Own Best Friend

A Children's Leadership Series

Limited Edition Coloring Book

Written by Kim Dawson

Illustrated by Paige Anocibar

Copyright by Kim Dawson

Publisher: Tandem Services Press
PO Box 220, Yucaipa, CA 92399
www.tandemservicesink.com

Book Design by Paige Anocibar

ISBN 978-1-954986-29-9

Appreciation to

Inland Leaders Charter School and all our teachers and staff for inspiring and supporting me to write this series.

All my students and their families who taught me to be a better teacher and person.

The 2nd grade, 4th grade, and 5th grade classes at Inland Leaders and Wildwood that gave me GREAT feedback and helped me make this story better!

Pelican Elementary in Oregon for letting us use their school as a model for Lexie's Huckleberry Elementary.

My family and friends who have never wavered in supporting and encouraging my mission to help others.

Paige, my illustrator, for putting up with my "creative" tangents.

Jennifer Crosswhite, my editor and friend, who has been my sounding board and always keeps me positive when I hit the many bumps in the road. (https://www.tandemservicesink.com)

All my readers who have supported me and helped me spread the message that kids can be leaders too.

Sending a ton of love and encouragement to all of you!
We got this!

From the author of the series Living Love Forward:

I wrote this children's leadership series to create an open conversation about the experiences our kids face every day. Being a teacher for over two decades, I have created connections with kids of all ages. I have observed and learned a lot through these interactions and have discovered key skill sets that I think are important for their growth. My purpose in writing these sentimental and caring stories is the hope that they instill life skills and resilience in our children. In turn, this empowers them to become successful and compassionate people, as well as strong leaders. Join Lexie and our children as they navigate this journey of self-discovery.

Please note that this series can be used in conjunction with any Leadership Program focused on survival skills and effective habits for children.

This book specifically focuses on:

- **Anxiety**
- **Frustration**
- **Hyperactivity**
- **Name calling**
- **Negative attitude**
- **Poor coping skills**
- **Poor self-esteem**

Map of Harlow

Train Station

Church of Hope

Cemetery

Liberty Library

Lexie's House

Bus Stop

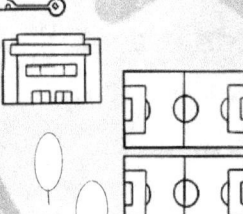

Jackson Sports Park

Riverside Park

Annabelle's House

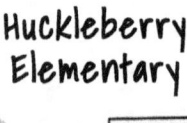
Huckleberry Elementary

1st Street

2nd Street

2nd Street

4th Street

Main Street

Main Street

Main Street

Rose Road

Rose Road

Lavender Lane

Lavender Lane

Lavender Lane

Jasmine Avenue

Jasmine Avenue

Lotus Lane

2nd Street

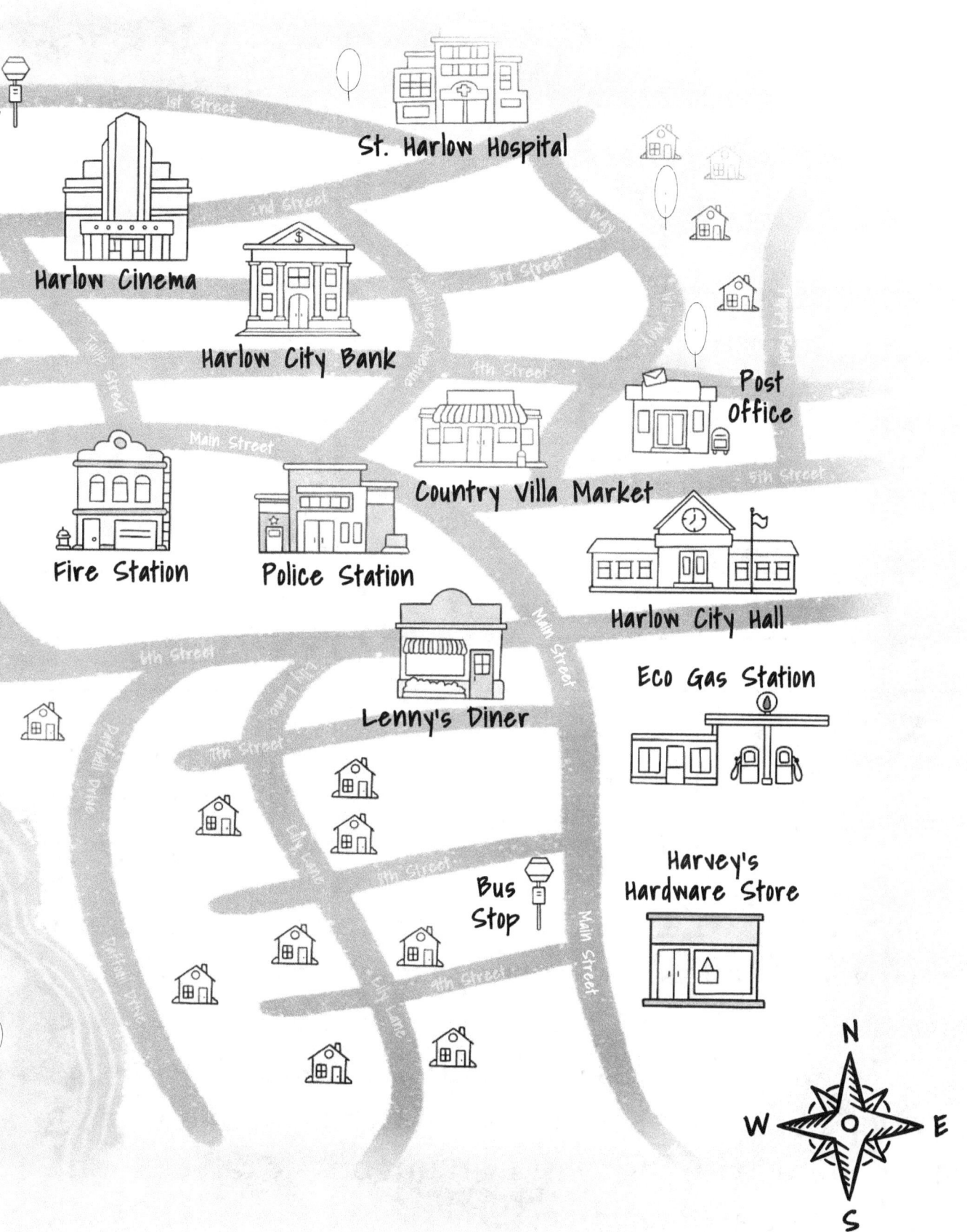

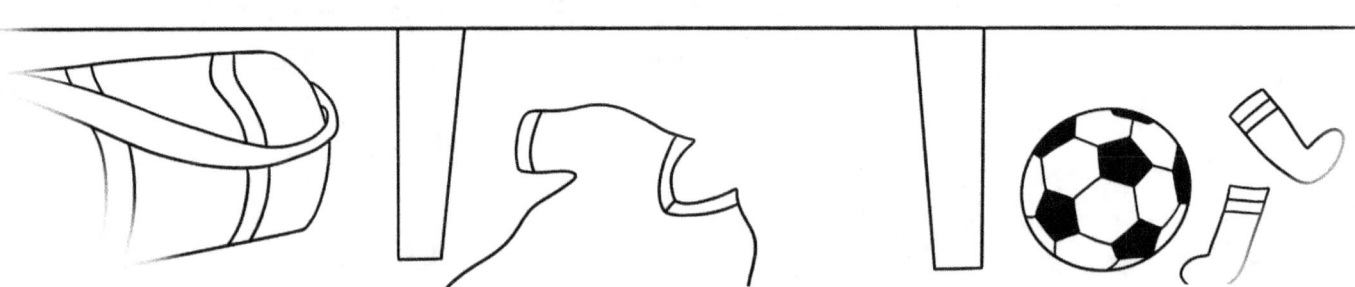

"Sam, watch where you are going! You almost knocked me over!" I yell as Sam races past me into the dining room.

He drops into his chair and mumbles, "Sorry, Lexie." He dumps some cereal into a bowl and starts to eat it along with the toast Dad put on the table. Soon, he gets distracted by his tablet.

"Sam, quit messing around and finish your breakfast! We are going to miss your soccer game. Come on, you guys! We gotta go!" Dad shouts as he holds open the door. Sam, a nervous ball of energy, rushes through the door and out to the car. Dad and I follow. I laugh at Sam as he races to the car, juggling the rest of his toast, water bottle, soccer bag, and ball

Sam sighs and **anxiously** waits for Dad to unlock the car door. "Take a breath, Sam. Everything is going to be ok," Dad reassures him.

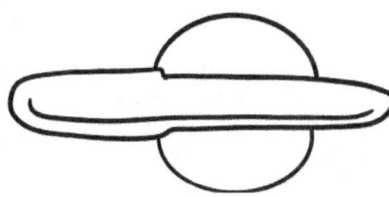

Sam grumbles something under his breath, as he gets into the car. He is restless but finally does settle down and sits quietly in his seat. Today is a big game for him and depending on how it goes decides if the team goes to the playoffs. He munches on his toast as we drive towards the field.

As Dad and I set up our chairs I glance over to Sam as he warms up for his game. I can see how nervous he is feeling. He is playing the forward position in the game. As a forward, Sam usually makes the most goals during the games.

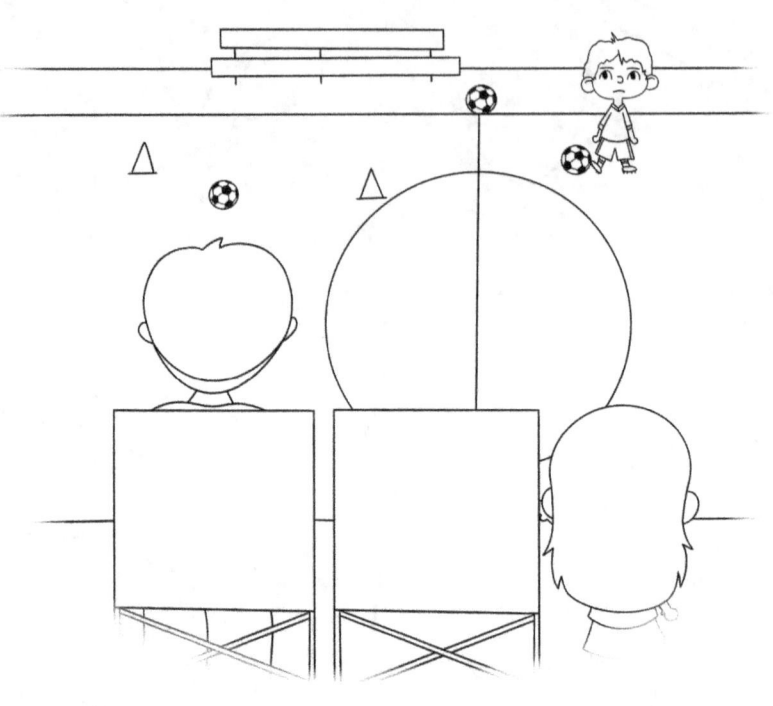

Sam is **criticized** a lot for never slowing down, but the soccer field is one place where all of his extra energy makes him a better player.

The game starts and he gets the ball. I start yelling
when I see him weaving in and out of the other team's
players who are guarding the goal. He dribbles and
shoots, but their goalie knocks the ball out of bounds.
This happens over and over again, each time he tries
to score he misses.

He can't seem to get the ball in the net today and I can see the **frustration** on his face. Sam is off today and he isn't playing like he usually does. Despite this, his team wins by one point. They are in the playoffs! Everyone is celebrating but Sam. I see him off to the side of the field, frowning with his head down.

"Way to go, Sammy Boy!" Dad says after the game. He gives him a big hug and pats him on the back. Sam slightly smiles at him and they begin to walk to the car. I notice he is quiet all the way home. This stillness is unusual for Sam.

The next day, I notice that Sam seems upset and I ask him about it. At first, he mumbles that he doesn't want to talk about it, but after I **pester** him for a while, he abruptly starts talking.

Throwing himself on the couch, he takes a deep breath, rolls his eyes, and looks at me angrily. "I am not good at anything, Lexie!" he yells. "I can barely read! I am always getting into trouble because I am always moving around! I even screwed up during the game yesterday, because I couldn't make any goals!"

I see how upset he is and I try to think of what Dad would say if he were here. I remember a time when I was down on myself too. Dad had found me crying in the bathroom. When he asked what was wrong, I remember sobbing and saying, "Annabelle is so much prettier than me. I am ugly, Dad. I am dumb too! I stink in math, so I am in the low group during math class!" I explain.

I look down at Sam sitting on the couch. I lean toward him and tell him what Dad had said to me. I said, "Sam, you have to become your own best friend."

Sam responds with, "What are you talking about?"
I reply, "Sam, if your best friend had said that he wasn't good at anything and that he was dumb, what would you say to him?"

Sam thought for a minute. Finally, he said, "I would tell him not to say that about himself. No one is perfect and he shouldn't be mean to himself like that."

I tell Sam, "Dad calls that **self-bullying...** and self-bullying is never ok. The things we say to ourselves in our head should be positive and make us feel better. When we are down, we need to lift ourselves back up and not wait for anyone else to do it for us, right? Isn't that what Dad is always telling us?"

With a sigh, Sam nods.

"Sam, when things get **rough** and you start to hear yourself saying mean things in your head, try doing this... Ask yourself what would you say if it was your best friend saying those mean things about himself. Whatever positive and **honest** reply you give him should be the **advice** you take for yourself."

I tell Sam again, "You need to be your own best friend!" Then I reach out and laughingly push his arm. He grabs me and we fall to the floor laughing and wrestling. I can tell he is feeling better, especially after he throws couch pillows at me.

At school on Monday, Sam is reading a story with his teacher in class. He struggles with some of the words and starts to get upset. In his head, he starts to self-bully and is thinking, "Mrs Clement is going to think you are dumb! The other kids can do this, so why can't you?"

This time, however, Sam catches himself. He lifts his head and looks at his teacher. "Mrs. Clement, will you help me? I am struggling with some of the words, but one day I WILL read better. I just have to keep trying," he says to her.

She smiles down at him and says, "I have never doubted you. Just because you are struggling in reading doesn't mean you are not a smart boy. You are super smart! Remember, Sam, no one is perfect. We all struggle somewhere. That makes you perfectly imperfect just like the rest of us and I think you are doing great! Now, let's finish this story together." Sam smiles and starts to read with a new confidence in himself.

Author's Advice

- Don't self-bully and say negative things to yourself.

- It is ok to be perfectly imperfect.

- If you say something negative and mean to yourself, stop, and say something positive and nice instead.

- It is normal to feel frustrated and anxious at times even adults can feel this way.

- If you wouldn't want your best friend saying it about themselves... you shouldn't be saying it to yourself... be your own best friend.

Think and Feel

Look at page 7. Have you ever found yourself in a similar situation? Did you self-bully? Would you do anything differently if you were to relive that experience? If so, what would you do different?

Glossary

advice

Definition: an idea or opinion offered as help in making a choice or a decision.

Part of Speech:

This word is a (**noun**, adjective, verb, adverb).

Evidence of how the word is used in the story.

Lexie gives Sam advice (an idea) about how to be kinder to himself.

anxiously

Definition: feeling worried, nervous, or afraid about something uncertain.

Part of Speech:

This word is a (noun, adjective, verb, **adverb**).

Evidence of how the word is used in the story.

Sam waits anxiously (full of worry and nervousness) for Dad to open the car door so they can go to his important soccer game.

Glossary

criticized

Definition: to put down and be judged as bad: to find fault with

Part of Speech:

This word is a (noun, adjective, verb, adverb).

Evidence of how the word is used in the story.

Sam is criticized (put down and judged) for having a lot of energy, but when he plays soccer that extra energy is looked at as a good thing, not a bad thing.

frustration

Definition: the feeling of being upset or annoyed, especially because of an inability to change or do something

Part of Speech:

This word is a (noun, adjective, verb, adverb).

Evidence of how the word is used in the story.

Lexie can see the frustration (annoyance) on Sam's face because he can't make a goal. He keeps trying but the ball misses the net or is grabbed by the goalie.

Glossary

honest

Definition: truthful, real, or sincere

Part of Speech:

This word is a (noun, **adjective**, **verb**, adverb).

Evidence of how the word is used in the story.

When Lexie is helping Sam, she talks about being positive and honest (truthful) with yourself and not just negative.

pester

Definition: to bother again and again

Part of Speech:

This word is a (noun, adjective, **verb**, adverb).

Evidence of how the word is used in the story.

Lexie knows something is bothering Sam, so she pesters (bothers or bugs him) until he tells her what is wrong.

Glossary

rough

Definition: when things are hard to deal with: not polite or kind or easy to handle

Part of Speech:

This word is a (noun, **adjective**, verb, adverb).

Evidence of how the word is used in the story.

When Lexie is trying to help Sam stop self-bullying, she says that when times are rough (hard to deal with) switch the negative thoughts with positive ones.

self-bullying

Definition: to hurt yourself by saying mean things to yourself

Part of Speech:

This word is a (noun, adjective, **verb**, adverb).

Evidence of how the word is used in the story.

When Sam is picking on himself and calling himself dumb, he is self-bullying (hurting himself).

About the Author: Kim Dawson

I am a single mom of two wonderful kids. I have been teaching for a number of decades and love spending time with my students. I have been writing since I was a child. It has always been a way for me to express myself when I am struggling. I strongly believe that we do not give our kids the credit they deserve. They have a lot to teach us if we just listen.

About the Illustrator: Paige Anocibar

Art is my passion. Every day I am thankful to have a career that empowers me to express myself through creativity. Drawing has been a part of my life since I was a small child. Coloring and painting were my favorite part of going to school. Back then, just like now, I was eager for the next art project. I knew that expressing myself through art is all I have ever wanted to do with my life, and illustrating this book has helped me achieve a part of that dream.

If you enjoyed this story, see other books in this Children's Leadership series, Living Love Forward.

2023 Books

February

May

September

November

2024 Books

February

May

September

November

www.ingramcontent.com/pod-product-compliance
Lightning Source LLC
Chambersburg PA
CBHW081346120626
46546CB00011B/3468